# Self-Care
## from Body to Bliss

Also by Jane M. Mayer

*Helping Mom*
*The Accidental Caregiver Series*
*Helping Others Without Losing Yourself*

# Self-Care
## from Body to Bliss

*The Accidental Caregiver Series*

*Helping Others Without Losing Yourself*

## Jane M. Mayer

SWEET JANE LLC

2024

*Self-Care from Body to Bliss*
*The Accidental Caregiver Series*
*Helping Others Without Losing Yourself*
Jane M. Mayer

This book provides general information and discussions
about health and related subjects. The information and other
content provided in this book, or in any linked materials, are
not intended and should not be construed as medical or legal
advice, nor is the information a substitute for professional
medical expertise or treatment.

Foreword by Kamini Desai, PhD
Editor: Stacey Dyck
Cover/Book Design: Margi Levitt

Published by Sweet Jane LLC • www.sweetjaneslife.com
ISBN: 979-8-9900080-2-1 (ebook)
ISBN: 979-8-9900080-3-8 (paperback)

For everyone
who dares to peel back the layers
and dive deeply inside.

"To love oneself
is the beginning of a
lifelong romance."

*– Oscar Wilde*

# Contents

# Foreword

IN THE JOURNEY OF LIFE, there are often unexpected twists and turns that lead us down paths we never imagined traversing. For some, this includes the role of caregiver – an unforeseen responsibility that can alter the course of one's life in profound ways. The path can be a challenging one. It can be a challenge that defeats us, or a challenge that hones us into the person we can become. Mayer offers us a glimpse into the latter.

In *The Accidental Caregiver Series – Helping Others Without Losing Yourself*, Jane M. Mayer offers a compassionate and insightful exploration of the caregiver experience.

With wisdom gleaned from her own journey and years of study and practice in yoga and wellness, Mayer provides a roadmap for caregivers navigating the delicate balance between caring for others and caring for oneself.

Walking the path of caregiving requires an immense amount of strength, resilience, and love – especially when faced with the complexities of health challenges, aging, or disability. But amidst the demands of caregiving, it is all too easy to neglect one's own needs, leading to burnout, exhaustion, and a sense of lost identity.

What sets this series of books apart is Mayer's holistic approach to self-care, which recognizes that true well-being encompasses not only the physical body but also the energetic, mental/emotional, wisdom, and bliss bodies. By addressing each of these dimensions, caregivers can cultivate a deeper sense of balance, vitality, and inner peace, even in the midst of adversity. We can become greater for having had the experience of caregiving and find ourselves maturing through it.

Through practical strategies, and self-care practices addressing the total person, Mayer empowers caregivers to prioritize their own well-being and reclaim their sense of self amidst the demands of caregiving. She reminds us that self-care is not selfish but rather essential for sustainable caregiving and maintaining healthy relationships with those we care for.

As you embark on this journey through *The Accidental Caregiver Series*, may you find solace, inspiration, and practical guidance to navigate the complexities of caregiving with grace and resilience. May you discover new depths of compassion, strength, and self-awareness within yourself, and may you emerge from this experience with a renewed sense of purpose and vitality.

With deep gratitude to Jane M. Mayer for shining a light on the path of caregiving and offering invaluable support and guidance to caregivers everywhere.

Kamini Desai, PhD

•••

Kamini Desai PhD is the author of *Yoga Nidra: The Art of Transformational Sleep* and is considered a leading authority on Yoga Nidra – a form of meditative self-care. As the creator of the I AM Yoga Nidra Training, and the I AM Being App, she uniquely combines the ancient wisdom of yoga with Western psychology and science.

Her father, the renowned Indian master Gurudev Shri Amritji brought the teachings of yoga to the U.S. in the 1960s and significantly enriched Western yoga with a deeper spiritual aspect.

Kamini has been teaching worldwide for over 35 years.
In 2012, she was awarded the title of Yogeshwari (woman of yogic mastery) for uniquely bringing ancient illumination to the real challenges of human experience.

"You yourself, as much as anybody in the entire universe, deserve your love and affection."

– *Buddha*

# The Layers of Our Being

I DEFINE AN ACCIDENTAL CAREGIVER *as a person who commits to looking after the well-being of another, either by choice or by circumstance, but who does not necessarily have training or professional experience to draw upon.*

Throughout my life, I have repeatedly found myself in this position. The joys, pitfalls, and strategies that I share in my Accidental Caregiver series come from my years of caring for others, while working to maintain a peaceful life of my own.

It can be daunting to create and maintain a steady, happy existence at any time, let alone when faced with the overwhelming responsibilities of caregiving. I've learned that it can be done, though, with consistent effort, a commitment to oneself, and a bit of practice. Just like the mini tarts I create as a baker, these life guides are served up to be digested in small bites. They are designed as easy reads that just might spark a desire for further learning and growth.

*Self-Care from Body to Bliss* is the second in *The Accidental Caregiver* series. My hope is that by sharing my personal insight and experience, I can help caregivers look at self-care in a whole new way. One that addresses our many layers of being and works to soothe and strengthen all facets of our complex and wonderful selves.

With more than twenty years of study, practice, and personal and professional experience in the yoga and wellness industry, I have learned a thing or two about creating a peaceful way of being. One facet of ancient Eastern philosophy that has had a significant and lasting impact on my life and my conception of self-care, are the five Koshas. Kosha is a Sanskrit word meaning sheath or layer, and this 5000-year-old yogic theory is based on us, as human beings, having five layers of self:

1. Physical Body

2. Energetic Body

3. Mental/Emotional Body

4. Wisdom Body

5. Bliss Body

Each of these bodies have beautiful Sanskrit names and each are an education unto their own, in terms of the rich insight they contribute to our understanding of our true selves. For our purposes here, I want to explore how we can use this framework of the five Koshas to approach self-care in a way that benefits every layer of our being.

Imagine the human experience as a set of nesting dolls, with five layers or *shells* all connected into one. If you remove one layer, the next is revealed and so on, until the center of the doll – its core – is discovered. This is one way to visualize our own layers of being. The most tangible and obvious is the Physical Body, while the wisdom and bliss bodies are more subtle and elusive. Each layer is always present and the more they work in harmony, the closer you are to your highest and greatest self.

Even though each layer always exists, we aren't always aware of them. In fact, it's possible for someone to go through life without ever identifying or contemplating most of them! This can lead to a sense of disconnection that may be difficult to define or articulate, but that affects us in myriad ways, nonetheless. Practicing self-care in and among the five Koshas allows us to be reunited with our various selves and promotes a deep sense of wholeness and alignment.

Before diving in, I want to introduce an idea that you'll see throughout the guide.

$$\frac{Consistent\ Effort}{Time} = Results$$

I firmly believe that *being consistent*, with conscious awareness in your efforts, *over a sustained period*, will yield the *desired result*. Just like with any new habit or commitment, whether it's trying to manage your weight or improve a relationship, it takes time for self-care to be embedded into our day-to-day routines. As much as it is meant to be enjoyable, making it happen isn't without effort. It requires us to prioritize ourselves, set time aside and use that time wisely, and believe that our health and well-being is worth our care and attention.

•••

You will notice that I use the term 'results' instead of 'successes'. Pursuing a desired outcome rather than just aiming for success helps us focus on the journey rather than fixating on the destination. If we solely chase the weighted and subjective notion of success, we end up on the hamster wheel, striving for superficial gains, often experiencing disappointment, and never feeling truly satisfied because the goal posts keep moving.

While it's natural to seek tangible rewards for our efforts, we can find satisfaction without labeling our experiences as "failures" or "successes." Every setback is an opportunity for growth. I encourage my yoga teachers-in-training to recognize that simply showing up for class is a significant achievement in itself. We can extend this same compassion to ourselves, showing up and doing our best without struggling under arbitrary measures.

Self-care is a bit of a buzz word these days and is often used synonymously with pampering, like taking a bubble bath or getting our nails done. Believe me, I'm here for that! I have found, however, that there are additional approaches and means of self-care that offer deeply fulfilling ways to soothe the mind and enrich the soul.

Let's explore all of these, starting with the Physical Body.

"Sometimes the most important thing in a whole day is the rest we take between two deep breaths."

*– Etty Hillesum*

1

*Self-Care for the Five Bodies*

# Physical Body

IT'S PRETTY EASY TO IDENTIFY and acknowledge one's Physical Body, given that it is the vehicle that rolls us out of bed each morning and stares back at us in the mirror.

Each of us is a unique and beautiful individual and effective self-care techniques and practices are not one-size-fits-all. What may be uplifting for one may be inaccessible or unappealing to another. Even so, I believe that the following approaches to caring for our physical bodies are pretty much universally applicable – in one variation or another – and worth exploring.

## ACCEPTANCE

Self-acceptance is the first step in creating a healthy body. Although it may feel counter-intuitive, honoring who we are *in this moment* is the only surefire way to get and stay healthy. Spending our precious energy comparing, striving, and working to change our bodies, from a place of thinking that we are not good enough, will only leave us exhausted, unsatisfied, and deeply unhappy.

I used to work in advertising as a commercial producer. Most of our clients were in the fashion and cosmetic industries, and I often found myself accompanying models in the backseat of limousines on our way to shoot commercials. It was incredible to me how often these virtual goddesses, with their ocean blue eyes and porcelain skin, would spend our commute tearing themselves down or worrying about how they didn't measure up to their fellow models. How could someone so undeniably gorgeous be so dissatisfied with their looks?

These experiences, among many others, taught me that we each have our own barometer of acceptance for our physical self, and how we believe the world perceives us is impossibly subjective. If we measure our level of awesomeness on how we think others see us, we will never be satisfied as there is always a new standard to meet and new comparisons to make.

As a yoga instructor, my students would often ask me when they would be able to touch their toes, or hold a balance, or achieve the perfect headstand. My answer would inevitably be, "As soon as you stop trying so hard." Not the response anyone wants to hear, and again frustratingly counter-intuitive, but it is that very grasping at something you are not that keeps change and growth out of reach! In other words, if we accept ourselves as we are, we also accept the journey toward our future self, and allow achievements and change to come in their own way, on their own time.

Practicing self-acceptance is one of the most powerful ways that you can take care of your Physical Body. There are many ways of promoting self-acceptance, and different methods work for different people.

*Body Positivity*

Staring into the mirror and complimenting yourself (yes, out loud) on the body standing before you can be life-affirming and life-changing. Why do we find it so easy to accept and believe negative feedback and critique, while it is almost impossible for us to accept and internalize positive and affirming comments, from both ourselves and others? What if we directed the same amount of energy that we use to lament our fleshy arms (yes, that's me) to celebrate and thank those same arms for being strong, capable, and allowing us to hug those we love? Our bodies are our most trusted, longest-term companions. What do we achieve by tearing them down?

*Positive Thinking*

The Sanskrit phrase *pratipaksha bhavana* (pra-tee-pahk-sha bah-vah-nah) translates to *opposite emotion* or *sentiment*. When our mind locks onto a negative thought, we can draw on *pratipaksha bhavana* to flip the script. Instead of allowing the negative thought to embed itself, try to recognize its presence and think, or even better say, the exact opposite.

Along these same lines, on the days that I wake up with a general sense of negativity, I force a slight smile on my face and consciously work to keep it there all day. I don't know exactly how it works, but somehow the energy of the smile seems to create a mental shift and my mood almost invariably improves and lightens. A sub-conscious version of 'fake it until you make it'!

*Celebrate Your Unique Qualities*

I once had the opportunity to hear a keynote speaker at a graduation ceremony for a prestigious university. As he surveyed the privileged group of accomplished students, he cautioned them about not acting superior to others. Instead, he encouraged them to adopt a sense of humility and reminded them, "Everyone you meet knows something you don't."

No matter what our personal context or circumstance, each of us has a unique set of talents, abilities, strengths, and interpersonal assets. By taking the time to consider and identify everything you bring to the table, and keeping these qualities top of mind, you reinforce a positive sense of self and a renewed confidence while also practicing non-judgment toward others.

*Make Room for What You Cannot Change*

We are often told to accept or *let go* of the things we cannot change. It's good advice and self-acceptance certainly includes making peace with *what is*. But letting go can be hard, if not impossible, and for some things, a more attainable strategy might be to *make room for what we cannot change*.

Many years ago, I was going through a heartbreak. A relationship that was not meant to be had ended, and I was consumed by grief. I tried for weeks, then months, then *years*, to let go of the heartache, but it just wasn't working. Finally, I decided that I needed to try something different. Rather than work to erase and deny these feelings that had become a part of my being, I decided to let them stay and to spend my energy accepting and learning how to live with them.

I created a visualization of my grief – a little camper who lived in my heart-space. He set up his tent, had his fire and backpack, and sat on a log in a position of deep sadness. I told him he could live there for as long as he needed but, in the meantime, I was going to focus on the rest of my life. I set to work finding things that brought me happiness and purpose, all the while acknowledging the little camper but trying to not dwell on him. Years went by as I focused on family, yoga, teaching, and my health. I would occasionally check in with my little camper, spend some time and feel the familiar twinge of heartache, and then move on with my day. These visits became less and less frequent, until one day, without notice, I realized that he had packed up his stuff and hiked away. The memories of the relationship were still there, but the heart-ache was gone. It took a long time, but it worked.

In life, there are things that we cannot control but the good news is that we have complete control over how we show up in the face of them.

## Be Kind to Yourself

Early in my yoga practice, I was encouraged to notice how kind or, more accurately, how unkind I was being to myself as I learned the postures and poses. The barrage of mental criti-cisms, comparisons, and critiques that I was laying on myself was truly eye-opening. I was then encouraged to consciously guide myself through the practice as I would a child. Helping a little one who was simply trying to do their best would require a completely different language and attitude, and I was to use that approach on myself. The result? My internal monologue was much more patient, kind, and focused on promoting feelings of safety and confidence. What a difference! Why do we feel it's okay to treat ourselves in ways that we would never treat others?

A yoga master once shared this quote with me: *Every time you judge yourself, you break your own heart*. Being unkind to yourself chips away at your confidence and self-esteem. Giving yourself the space and patience to learn and grow through experience is a constant act of love. The more you love yourself, the more love you have to give.

## FOOD

You'll notice that I use the word 'food' instead of 'diet'. The word 'diet' gives me anxiety as it evokes thoughts of deprivation and scarcity – the opposite of a happy, healthy life. I feel compelled to admit, however, that I have spent *years* dieting to lose weight or achieve a certain ideal. I have pinballed between dieting and a healthy approach to eating most of my life but am proud to have finally found a place of balance where I feel good, eat well, and accept who I am, as I am.

It seems to me that there are two types of people in the world when it comes to food. Those who eat to live and those, like me, who live to eat. When I contemplate indulging in something decadent, I remind myself that I am not striving for an epitaph of *Here lies Jane, known for her outstanding ability to deny herself pleasure*. Quite the opposite, in fact. I plan to spend my last days reviewing and reliving my extensive culinary adventures, with smiles and contented sighs.

After a lifetime of trying to manage my relationship with food through plans, restrictions, charts, lists, groups and apps, I am *done*. I've embraced the simplicity of:

1. Eat when hungry.

2. Stop when full.

3. Eat food that grows from the earth.

4. Focus on proteins, vegetables, and complex carbohydrates.

5. Enjoy the experience.

6. Indulge sometimes.

7. Share mealtimes with others.

While I unabashedly delight in all things delicious, I also appreciate the food-as-medicine approach and believe that healthy choices can be satisfying and sustaining. Whatever approach resonates with the kindest and most caring version of yourself is likely the one you should stick with it.

## MOVEMENT

By now, you've undoubtedly noticed that I believe the words we use matter. In this case, I prefer the term *movement* to *exercise*. Exercise carries certain connotations and not everyone is up for a 'workout', whereas we can all move our Physical Body to some degree, even if it's with assistance.

My 98-year-old mother's regime includes sitting in her recliner and circling her feet, flexing and pointing her toes, wiggling her fingers, and using the chair to help her flatten out and stretch her spine. Movement. This regime is what is available and appropriate for Mom, and it helps her connect to her Physical Body.

My fitness trainer is on the opposite end of the spectrum. She is a pint-sized powerhouse who teaches and trains at the gym every day and competes in and wins cross-fit and weight-lifting competitions. Movement. For her, it is a lifestyle and how she connects to and celebrates her Physical Body.

Most of us likely fall somewhere between these two extremes. No matter where you are on the mobility spectrum, it's hard to argue the importance of movement in maintaining our bodies, promoting well-being, and staying energized and youthful. Movement boosts our mood, helps with concentration and digestion, promotes restful sleep, and improves our cardiovascular and overall physical health.

Taking a short walk every day (dogs are great motivation!), stretching when you wake up, making time for an exercise video or class, visiting your neighborhood park for a pickleball game, or hitting the gym a few times a week, are all ways that we can keep our bodies moving and honor this vehicle that takes us through life.

The best way to move your body is to do the thing that feels good. You may have to work at sticking with it in the beginning but if you've landed on the right type of movement, you will soon start to look forward to it and see it as more of a blessing than a chore.

## BODY CARE

For me, body care often involves massage therapy, steam showers, pedicures, facials, and trips to the salon. While these may fall under the banner of pampering, they have important ripple effects on my emotional state, confidence, and overall health.

I firmly believe that physical self-care is a worthwhile investment but there are many ways to maintain a healthy physical self without breaking the bank. A simple home facial done a couple of times a month, or even just using a favorite scented body cream, can make us feel like we are caring for ourselves and that we matter.

Other ways that I take care of my body include using healthy hair and skin products, annual visits to medical professionals like the dermatologist, connecting with my naturopath, getting my yearly woman's wellness check, taking vitamins and supplements, and wearing sunscreen.

It's so important that we don't wait until our bodies break down or cry out for attention, but proactively listen to and address the messages they send us. It is much easier to create a habit of preventative care than suffer the physical, financial, and emotional consequences of having to fix what's broken.

Whatever your routine, be sure to make it affordable, sustainable, and enjoyable. I am grateful for my one body, and I appreciate it as a trusted companion who is with me from the beginning to the end. Let's be good to our bodies and they will be good to us.

•••

## CONSISTENT EFFORT OVER TIME = RESULTS
*Five Step Strategy to Self-Care for the **Physical Body***

### *Set an Intention*

Experiment with letting go of goal setting and explore *setting intentions* instead. For example, you could re-frame a goal of losing 20 pounds in six months into an intention of moving your body every day and being conscientious about the healthy food you eat. In six months, it is highly likely that your body will have responded to your intentional shift, without the mental burden of striving to reach a goal. Instead of trying to make something happen, show up with consistent effort and simply *let* it happen.

### *Create a Routine*

Integrating a daily routine to support an intention does not need to be difficult, it just takes some commitment at the outset. The routine can be simple. It could be something that improves your environment, such as making the bed and straightening your room each day, or that benefits your

Physical Body, such as a daily walk. It might be regularly taking vitamins or supplements, or always bringing a water bottle when you leave the house. Try to stick with the ones you choose for at least six months to notice the feeling of your focused accomplishment. When you inevitably fall from the path, take notice, smile at the perfection of how human you are, and step back into the routine.

### Stay Accountable

Once you have set your intention and created a routine, the next step is to show up 100% for yourself, whatever that means on a given day. This can be challenging as life happens and our focus strays. Accountability is the key to sustainability. I meet with my personal trainer twice a week to achieve my intentions of increasing strength and staying at a healthy weight. Am I capable of doing a routine without her? Yes. Do I show up for myself consistently? No. Declaring your intentions to someone, or journaling each day to report on your actions, are also good ways to hold yourself accountable.

### Avoid Comparisons

I remember a time when I was working out regularly, teaching yoga classes, and feeling pretty good about my life and physical state. That was until I spotted a magazine cover featuring a celebrity, who was my same age, sporting a bikini and promoting her astounding career trajectory. I suddenly felt less than awesome, not to mention irrelevant and unaccomplished.

Comparison kills happiness and social media hasn't helped. Limiting your time on socials and remembering that we are all running our own race (full of challenges and stresses not shared on our highlight reels) are two ways to avoid crashing your self-esteem.

### Celebrate the Results

I believe that celebrating tiny wins and acknowledging baby steps are key to living with big energy and lots of satisfaction. It's a matter of redefining success to see that achievement is simply a series of little things, meaning that the little things are in fact the big things! Regularly rewarding yourself with enjoyable gifts or experiences can make the difference between maintaining consistency or giving up. I have a love affair with lip gloss, so I often reward my efforts (whatever they may be) with a new shade. Ralph Waldo Emerson put forward that, "the reward for a thing well done is having done it", and I agree, but a new lip gloss works too!

"Beauty is how you feel inside, and it reflects in your eyes. It is not something physical."

*– Sophia Loren*

**2**

# Energetic Body

IF OUR PHYSICAL BODY IS THE VESSEL that carries us through this world, our Energetic Body is the electrical system that charges it. This energy layer is the life force of our being and is connected to the energy that surges through nature and the universe.

A tried-and-true technique of exploring and connecting with this part of our being is through breath work. As we breathe in, we take energy into our system, and as we breathe out, energy is released. We can manage, maximize, and manipulate our energy by focusing on and moderating our breath in specific ways to create different effects. For instance, slow steady breathing through the nose slows the heart rate and directs energy into the parasympathetic nervous system to create a calming effect. Conversely, breathing in and out through the mouth activates the sympathetic system, engaging the flight or fight response. Mouth breathing can energize the body but it can also add a sense of tension or stress to our experience.

Rest is a well understood cornerstone of energy management. We all know the powerful impact that a solid night's sleep has on our energy levels. While we sleep, our body is digesting, resetting, and processing, both mentally and physically. Even a short, 10-minute break with our eyes closed can do wonders. When rest isn't available to us, movement is a quick and effective way to boost our energy and create a sense of vibrancy.

Since becoming aware and in touch with my energetic self through my yoga practice and training, it has become an invaluable and life-transforming part of my daily experience. I've learned to connect with *prana*, the Sanskrit word for energy or *life force*, and in doing so have become connected to a place within and beyond me. By intentionally opening pathways for energy to flow through me, I've created within myself a portal to an energy center on which I have come to rely. The energy available to me through this pathway has a unique intelligence and I use it to help me navigate and understand the world.

Connecting to this internal energy pathway may sound a bit unusual but through paying close attention, I have witnessed energy move through my body and carry away that which was no longer serving me. I will explain this more fully later when I discuss somatic therapy as self-care for the Mental/Emotional Body.

Understanding and tapping into energy points and centers in the body takes time and knowledge. If you are interested in learning more about this type of energy work, seek out information on the chakras of the Ayurvedic system, and meridians and chi in the Chinese health culture. These would serve as a good introduction to what I consider a mind-blowing and life-changing practice.

•••

### CONSISTENT EFFORT OVER TIME = RESULTS
*Five Step Strategy to Self-Care for the **Energetic Body***

#### *Set an Intention*

A great initial intention would be to simply notice your daily breathing and explore shifting your breath from the chest to the belly (diaphragm). This can do wonders for your overall health. A next step might be to deepen the breath, as generated from the low belly center, in and out through the nose. This allows us to better manage our emotional response to stress, increases our energy and promotes mental clarity. You might set an intention of learning more, and there are many great books on conscious breathing (like *Breath* by James Nestor).

#### *Create a Routine*

Link your intention to an embedded routine, like while you wait for the coffee to brew or when sitting in the car at school pick-up. My smart watch reminds me, at a certain time every day, to pause what I'm doing and take some deep concentrated breathing. Even a once-a-day breath practice can improve wellness immeasurably.

### Stay Accountable

A journal or day-timer can be used to track how consistently you make time to breathe or meditate and is also a great place to record any observable or perceived changes or shifts. Seeing results is one of the best motivators for staying on course! You could also consider joining a weekly yoga or breath work class, as often the act of registration (and payment!) promotes accountability.

### Avoid Comparisons

There are different types of energy driven beings. In yogic philosophy, these are categorized as *tamasic*, *rajastic*, and *sattvic*. If you are someone who often feels lethargic or needs a little jump start to get going, you may be tamasic in nature. If you're quick to anger, passionate, ambitious, and high energy, you are likely more rajastic. A person who is generally even keeled and tends to stay calm when stressed might align with the sattvic persona. We all naturally possess a certain energetic personality, and the goal should be to accommodate and balance that which we are, with that which we need. It is self-defeating when we compare someone else's energetic routine with our own. Better to learn your own true nature and move into a lifestyle that balances YOU.

### Celebrate the Results

When you find yourself feeling relaxed, at ease and mentally clear, this is a great sign that your Energetic Body is getting what it needs. This is no small feat! Recognize this state of being and give yourself a moment to really bathe in the conscious awareness you've created. Try to identify what elements of your energetic practice have had the most impact on you and consider exploring those further. We call this, *following the feeling.*

"I have come to believe that caring for myself is not self-indulgent. Caring for myself is an act of survival."

*– Audre Lorde*

**3**

# Mental/Emotional Body

THE MENTAL/EMOTIONAL BODY is directed by the mind, and involves emotions, thoughts, triggers, brain chemistry and more. People spend their entire lives working to understand this aspect of our being, and since I am not a licensed psychologist, the following is simply what I can report from my personal experience as a practitioner, teacher, certified coach, and seeker.

## THERAPEUTIC COUNSELING

There have been periods in my life when I have sought counseling from a licensed therapist. Feeling stuck and disconnected can be debilitating and having a trained professional act as a sounding board and offer an objective perspective can be invaluable in getting through a trauma or even just sorting out the daily challenges of life.

Counseling is rarely a walk in the park. In my first go-around of therapy, a hot button topic came up that I wasn't ready to face, so I abandoned the effort and stopped attending the sessions. It took five years, but I eventually went back and found that I was ready to confront and address all the elements in my life that were no longer serving me (including that which had scared me off years before). Therapy can be wonderfully helpful, but it does require a level of openness and willingness and being ready to listen and receive comment from both your chosen professional and your own internal voice.

## SOMATIC THERAPY

Another form of energetic self-care is somatic therapy, a process which taps into the physical, energetic, and mental/emotional bodies at the same time. There are a variety of ways one can practice and be guided by somatic therapy. One version of this practice is done with the seeker holding a physical shape (like a yoga pose) with the support of a trained facilitator. While the physical body holds the posture, a specific dialogue is used to explore the blockages within the Mental/Emotional Body. The intent is to create energetic pathways through which unprocessed experiences can be released.

Somatic therapy was helpful for me after I successfully addressed some previously unresolved issues in traditional therapy. I found that while my Mental/Emotional Body had worked through them, the residual effects were still being held hostage in other layers of my physical being. Somatic therapy was dramatically effective in releasing these trapped feelings.

Even outside of somatic therapy, yoga can unveil truths about ourselves, sometimes when we least expect it. There have been many times over the years that I've had students abruptly leave the room during a yoga class, guided meditation, or teacher training session. Becoming aware of stored emotion and energetic blockages can be uncomfortable and even scary, but I know from experience that moving *through* the blockages is the only way to the other side. If you try to deny, compartmentalize, or push them down deep, they will very likely manifest themselves in other (possibly negative) ways at some point in our life.

## BELIEVING YOUR THOUGHTS

One of the biggest lessons I've learned through my own study, practice, and teaching around the Mental/Emotional Body, is when to believe and trust my own thoughts. As I often tell my students, *the mind has a mind of its own.* That is, thoughts come into our mental body spontaneously and without choice. Some thoughts are quite helpful, like the messages that guide us through putting on pants or riding a bike. These straightforward directives are based on experience and proven to be both safe and effective, so we can trust and follow through on them without too much thought.

Other thoughts that pop into our mind spontaneously, however, can be detrimental, unkind, irrelevant, and simply untrue. Criticisms like, "You will never amount to anything," or questionable advice like, "Sure, a fifth margarita is a great idea!" These notions are neither helpful, nor advisable for us to act upon, yet we default to believing them. Why? Because they come from that same smart mind that told us how to put on our pants!

The trick is knowing which messages to listen to and trust, and which to override because they are coming from a place that doesn't prioritize our health and wellness. This knowing is cultivated by practicing awareness. By contemplating and coming to understand that we have bodies, but we are not *just* our bodies. We have minds, but we are not *just* our minds. We have thoughts and feelings, but we are not *just* those thoughts and feelings.

Since time immemorial, philosophers, religious leaders and spiritual teachers have and will continue to expound on and dissect human's connections with our true selves. It can get pretty metaphysical but what I can report from my own experience, is that when we become self-aware, we start to create a different relationship with our thoughts, feelings, and actions. Life unfolds and we participate fully, but our *perspective* on life's events changes. Our experience is more that of being an audience to a play or movie, rather than being directly impacted by what's happening. When we can consciously witness ourselves, we achieve a greater sense of control and are able to consider our internal dialogue and the messages it sends us, from a calmer state.

## AWARENESS TECHNIQUE

One technique to gain some agency over the Mental/Emotional Body is to simply be aware of what's going inside of us. In practice, this means that when a negative thought or emotion arises, we can stop, acknowledge the feeling, take five deep breaths to steady the mind, and just notice what is happening in our body. You can ask yourself, "Are these thoughts helpful? Do they move me toward my highest good? Do they promote the well-being of myself or others?" If any of the answers are no, you may want to take a step back and re-frame the situation or recalibrate your reaction.

This type of awareness practice is just that, a practice. It can take years, if not a lifetime, to tame the mind and maintain control of our emotions. I credit yoga in all its forms for giving me the capacity to move from a place of *thinking and reacting*, to a place of *feeling and responding*, which I'm happy to report yields a much more positive and peaceful existence.

## FINANCIAL HEALTH

Most of us live in an environment where financial well-being is critical to our physical, mental, and emotional stability. My relationship to money has always had a major influence on my personal well-being. We didn't have a lot growing up and while we were always able to make ends meet, I recognize how the pervading sense of instability and insecurity has followed me throughout my life and shaped how I see and manage my family's finances.

Financial self-care comes from a sense of balance. When we are clear and honest with our current circumstance, live within our means, and understand goal setting and saving, we experience a greater sense of ease in our day-to-day lives.

I am by no means a financial expert, but what I can offer are the lessons I've learned along the way.

- *Create a budget:* I moved to NYC with $500 and a suitcase of clothes. I tracked every penny I spent, down to the cost of one subway token, because I knew that my survival depended on strict budgeting. I was able to make my starter salary cover my expenses, and to this day use a budget to stay on top of my spending.

- *Commit to saving:* My dad was so sweet and generous. One of those people who *if he had a nickel, he'd give you a dime.* Saving for a rainy day was not his forte. Even in my most meager times, I've tried to put some money into savings to provide a sense of security when things get tight.

- *Enjoy within your means:* How many times have you heard of someone working their whole life to fund a wonderful retirement, only to not live long enough to enjoy it? Financial well-being is a process of being honest with what you have and appreciating the value of those assets while you have them.

Spend some time thinking about what money means to you. For me, I've always known that money would not buy me happiness, but it would provide *opportunity.* Since becoming clear on what I wanted my money to help me achieve, I have consistently and intentionally allocated funds to my personal financial priorities. These include:

1. Create a sense of independence and security

2. Help others in need

3. Invest to create more wealth

There is an amazing documentary titled *Happy*, that explores what really makes human beings happiest in life. It underscores a truth I long suspected, that happiness and satisfaction are possible if we have our basic needs met. These are simply food, shelter, water, and meaningful connections. When we start pursuing more than what we truly need, our happiness tends to take a hit. Constantly comparing ourselves to others or striving for more can leave us feeling unsatisfied, no matter how much we've accumulated.

Having worked in industries defined by excess and luxury, I have seen this phenomenon firsthand. Some of my wealthiest clients and colleagues were plagued by feelings of emptiness and disappointment with their lives. From the outside they seemed to have it all–big apartments, vacation homes, luxury vehicles, and unbridled spending at restaurants and events. Their lack of true happiness, however, put it all in jeopardy as they sought out inappropriate relationships, self-medicated with drugs and alcohol, and worked all hours to avoid facing themselves.

In yogic philosophy, there is a tenant of 'non-hoarding'. This general principle is that all we really need to feel satisfied is what we can use in one day. In our consumer-driven society this concept feels impossible, but I know a few people who have chosen this lifestyle, and they are some of the happiest I've met.

•••

## CONSISTENT EFFORT OVER TIME = RESULTS
*Five Step Strategy to Self-Care for the* **Mental/Emotional Body**

### Set an Intention

Just as we can set intentions for our Physical Body, we can aspire to exercise our mind and gain agency over its wanton tendencies to run rampant and deliver messages that are questionable at best. An intention to promote awareness might be to notice your thoughts when you are in a state of heightened emotion. Rather that setting an unrealistic goal such as, "I will no longer get angry when driving," try to simply notice what thoughts jump to the forefront when you're behind the wheel. Identify the thoughts, even out loud to yourself, and describe them in a neutral way. It takes a good deal of practice to move from reacting to noticing, but over time you move through life in a much more peaceful way.

### Create a Routine

A great routine to implement when working to strengthen the Mental/Emotional Body is to write your thoughts and feelings down on a regular basis. Yes, journaling. Transferring the constant chatter from the mind onto the page does wonders for your emotional health. Another technique I enjoy is an end-of-the-day review with my partner when we each exchange the *highlights* and lowlights of the day. Sometimes it is just a quick list and we're done, other times it sparks bigger conversations that serve to help us process recent events.

### Stay Accountable

Enlisting another individual is always a good idea when you are establishing a consistent routine. It's so easy to cheat on yourself but less so when there is someone checking in on a regular basis. Sharing your intention and new routine with a counselor, friend, spouse, support group, or anyone you trust to hold space for you, can be a powerful step towards for positive change.

### Avoid Comparisons

Ruminating on why everyone else is happier than you are, or lamenting how others seem to navigate life with fewer trials and tribulations, is a recipe for disaster. We truly can't know the depth and complexity of anyone's life experience, and we know (though it begs repeating) that social media is an unreliable narrator. One helpful strategy is to sit quietly in meditation and ask yourself to remember a time when you felt completely at ease and content. Notice what bubbles up first. Seeking out more of whatever comes up is likely the path to fulfillment and meaning, even if it doesn't mirror the path being taken by anyone else.

### Celebrate the Results

One way to honor the investment you've made in your own emotional and mental well-being is to share your time and energy with the people around you. Some of the happiest people on earth are those who devote their lives to the service of others. You can also share your growth and everything you've learned with those who may benefit from the same. Establishing a genuine connection with someone through the sharing of vulnerabilities and positive progress is one of the most satisfying celebrations of all!

"If you restore balance in your own self, you will be contributing immensely to the healing of the world."

– *Deepak Chopra*

## 4

*Self-Care for the Five Bodies*

# Wisdom Body

A POPULAR WAY OF THINKING about the Wisdom Body is it being our "gut feeling." A deep knowing that is not generated from the conscious mind but from a place deeper inside, that sees and understands things that our other energy bodies can't. Often the messages from the Wisdom Body are different than those coming from the mental/emotional layer, but for me, wisdom trumps knowledge and learned behavior 100% of the time.

## KNOWING

I used to work with a group called Wounded Warriors that offered tools and strategies to veterans dealing with post-traumatic stress. The goal was to help them create a more peaceful day-to-day experience while dealing with strong and lingering memories. Once, after I'd introduced the concept of the Wisdom Body, a gentleman raised his hand with a question. He was a police officer and he described how occasionally when approaching a crime scene, he would feel the hairs on the back of his neck prickle. He took this to mean that something bad was in the offing and he should proceed with caution.

Was this his Wisdom Body coming through? Yes, friend. That's exactly what it was.

Have you ever met someone and taken an immediate liking to them? Or, conversely, met someone who just gave you a *bad feeling*? We don't often forget the latter. I remember one time, years ago, when I was at the grocery store with my toddler son. While holding him in my arms at the checkout line, he glanced at the innocent-looking young man bagging our groceries and declared, "I no like that guy." I was surprised and somewhat embarrassed and tried to coax him into more polite behavior. Knowing what I know now, I wonder if my son wasn't responding to something that he was picking up on a subconscious level.

## LISTENING

The Wisdom Body has proven to be the most powerful driving force of my being and my life. It has an intelligence all its own and one that extends far beyond my knowledge and learned behavior. My reverence for its power has led me to consciously cultivate my connection to it through listening. Listening sounds simple but it's so easy for messages to get drowned out by life, not to mention our noisy and intrusive ego.

To cultivate connection through listening, one must make a conscious effort to be still. Most of us don't know how to do this and we've become accustomed to living in a world that is increasingly fast-paced and frenetic. All this hustle and bustle means that we are continually missing the wise messages and information that our Wisdom Body is generating.

People tell me all the time that they have no concept of their Wisdom Body and wouldn't know how to listen to it if they did. This is a tricky one, but everything changed for me when I came to accept that:

*Our Wisdom Body is never wrong.*

This is a big, bold statement, I know. I believe it to be true and I also believe that we can FEEL wisdom. If we tune in enough, and trust ourselves enough, we will *feel* what is right. The more we care for our physical, mental/emotional, and energetic bodies, the better tuned in they will be to pick up on this inner wisdom and be ready to act from that place of knowing.

## TRUSTING

How do we know whether it is our conscience guiding us or the agenda of the ego? This is a MAJOR question and figuring it out how to navigate these conflicting waters can be life-altering.

The ego is constantly striving for that which it desires and avoiding that which it doesn't. It can be very persuasive and loud in its communications through our thoughts. The conscience, or our wisdom, doesn't have a greedy agenda and is driven only by helping us attain our highest good. In other words, everything you need is already within you and waiting patiently for you to listen and respond in kind.

*The ego speaks to you with words in your mind.*

*The conscience whispers in your heart.*

These whispers from your conscience, or your Wisdom Body, are ever-present, even while we go about the most mundane of our daily chores. Often in the grocery store, I will find myself compelled to pause and consider an item not on my list. I've learned that if I ignore the impulse and trust only what I wrote down, I will invariably get home to discover we needed that item after all! The Wisdom Body is with you through simple tasks like grocery shopping, to major life decisions about relationships and work. If we are aware and tuned in, and our other energy bodies are aligned and *in the flow*, all decisions become clearer and we can navigate life with better ease. We feel when we are grasping at life through the ego and can quickly recenter ourselves towards our highest good.

•••

## CONSISTENT EFFORT OVER TIME = RESULTS
*Five Step Strategy to Self-Care for the **Wisdom Body***

### *Set an Intention*

A good first step to living a life guided by wisdom is simply setting an intention to listen closely for the little voice inside you. Once you've become acquainted with the voice, and how it shares messages with you, you can work on following the advice and guidance shared. The 'right' choice often conflicts with the ego's agenda so it's advantageous to get to a place where you can act immediately on your inner knowing before your mind can pipe in and confuse the issue!

### Create a Routine

One of my go-to routines as it relates to my Wisdom Body is regularly setting aside time to ask myself a simple question and wait for the answer. Sometimes I am hoping for guidance on how to address a problem or issue that I am facing, while other times I am at a mental crossroad and need insight as to the right direction to take. I listen for the very first answer that bubbles up, and I write it down. I then repeat the question-and-answer routine two more times. That first response is the one from the Wisdom Body. You want to write it down immediately because once your mind and ego become aware of it, it will invariably be reconsidered, analyzed, and managed through default patterns. Making a habit of exercising this "wisdom muscle" and trusting the answer as it is revealed to you, will help you act in a way that serves you best.

### Stay Accountable

It's so easy to get caught listening to the ego's agenda and making decisions that don't serve you, even once you've committed to listening for and following your gut. If you have a life partner, trusted friend, family member, or even a paid professional, with whom you can share your wisdom journey, your level of accountability will increase exponentially.

By articulating your efforts to move from thinking and reacting, to feeling and responding, you will gain a different perspective on the experience. The person you tell can also act as a mirror for your behavior and you can ask them to watch for and let you know of any shifts and changes they observe as you move through the process.

### *Avoid Comparisons*

I had a yoga student years ago who, at the young age of thirteen, had turned to drugs and alcohol to self-medicate. Though they had overcome their addiction, the experience had left them emotionally stunted – feeling stuck in adolescence while being expected to function as an adult. Despite their consistent and earnest efforts to embody a physical and philosophical yoga practice, they were unable to connect with their Wisdom Body and had no sense of a gut instinct. They found it frustrating that others around them, including those they considered to be less dedicated students of the practice, seemed to connect with their inner knowing so much more easily. They were underestimating the impact of their trauma and life experience and forgetting that everyone has their own perfect timing on how and when these connections will be made. Striving to be like another literally blocks the pathway for that connection to be realized. We must remember that results will come, all in our own time, in our own way.

### *Celebrate the Results*

The feeling of being connected to your True Nature, as expressed in the Wisdom Body, is worth celebrating! In those moments when you experience freedom from being driven and dragged by your own ego, or that you recognize the amazing benefits and positivity that comes from leading your life from a place of knowing, share it with the world! Healthy behavior and happiness are contagious. Surround yourself with like-minded people who share the same energy and reinforce your ability to discern what your best self needs from what your ego mind wants. Your synergy will help to create more of the same!

"Breathe. Let go. And remind
yourself that this very moment
is the only one you know
you have for sure."

*– Oprah*

5

*Self-Care for the Five Bodies*

# Bliss Body

THE FIFTH AND FINAL energy layer of being is the Bliss Body. This is the least tangible of the five bodies and requires us to dive a little deeper into the spiritual realm.

**FEELING**

The Bliss Body is the bridge between our human experience and the ethereal one. The best way for us to connect to and experience the Bliss Body is through our feeling centers, and following the feelings that arise and accompany our everyday living.

Some of us have experienced those all-too-rare moments when we are so entranced by what we're doing that we are transported out of space and time. This is bliss. When the dancer merges into the dance, when the artist becomes the art, when the runner enters the zone, when two people dissolve into a kiss.

I like to work with ceramics and I used to escape my stressful job in NYC by visiting a local art studio on the weekends. Amazingly, a state of bliss was waiting for me every time I sat down at the pottery wheel. I'd arrive first thing in the morning and before I knew it, the sun was going down. I had been completely lost in the process of creating and would only become aware of my sore hands and aching arms once I was back home. It was heavenly.

Bliss requires a merging of the self with the experience, and we call this *integration*. When what we are doing matches what we are thinking, and both are in alignment with what we are feeling, a powerful connection is created. It doesn't only happen during creative endeavors, either. Integration can happen anywhere, like when playing golf or even doing the dishes! Being integrated with what we do is being absorbed in the moment to moment of life as it unfolds. A challenging yet worthy practice to explore.

## GATEWAY TO HAPPINESS

The messages we receive when connected to our Bliss Body are very important because these are our gateways to happiness. Self-care as it relates to the Bliss Body is simply connecting with it as often as possible, and in doing so, spending more and more time existing in a state of total integration, unity, and peace. The more time we spend there, the more the benefits will begin to seep effortlessly into our everyday.

A powerful means for me to connect to the Bliss Body has been through guided meditation. This method is different than solitary meditation, a practice that usually involves sitting in still and silent concentration for a period of time. This approach can be very challenging even for a well-practiced participant. In guided meditation, you lie down and simply follow the guidance of a facilitator (either live or recorded) who takes you on a journey through the five layers – physical, energetic, mental/emotional, wisdom and eventually into a state of bliss.

One approach to guided meditation is Yoga Nidra, meaning yogic sleep, and it is a powerful way to connect to the Bliss Body. This practice encourages a state of being, somewhere between wakefulness and sleep, that offers an opportunity to release long-held blockages and promotes a sense of wholeness and fulfillment.

Some time ago I produced a series of Yoga Nidra meditations in a sound studio. About halfway through my reading the scripts, the engineer cut in and said that we had to start again because he had drifted off to a different place. Living proof of how powerful these techniques can be!

The Bliss Body is always present, supporting you and holding you in a place of safety and love. It is not a realm to which we reach outward and draw in, or a state of being to achieve. It is a part of who and how we are, ready to envelop us each and every time we connect to it.

•••

## CONSISTENT EFFORT OVER TIME = RESULTS

*Five Step Strategy to Self-Care for the **Bliss Body***

### Set an Intention

To move into a space that seems elusive or intangible, sometimes the best intention we can make is to simply open ourselves up to the possibility that it exists at all. I intentionally stay open to the possibility of the great unknowns, such as reincarnation, and will verify their validity if and when I encounter them.

### Create a Routine

A strong routine of self-care for the Bliss Body is to establish a steady meditation practice. Meditation can take many forms, including something as simple as waking to watch the sun rise, taking a few breaths and just being still for a minute or two. Sitting in meditation has many, many variations and it is a worthy effort to explore them with in-person or online guidance to feel what resonates with your personality and ability. My favorite practice, as I mentioned, is Yoga Nidra. If you'd like to try one, you can find my Yoga Nidra recordings on my website at https://sweetjaneslife.com/meditations.

### Stay Accountable

A meditation practice lends itself perfectly to a journaling experience. Jotting down how you feel before and after can reveal quite a lot about your state of mind and body. Meditation can be a revelatory experience where the mind, in taking a break from thinking, is able to rewrite and reroute long-held habits, feelings and even traumas. Sharing your personal experiences and enlightenment journey with a facilitator, friend or another seeker can be very helpful in staying accountable to the routine and processing everything that comes up.

### Avoid Comparisons

A person's spiritual practice is as personal and unique as the individual themselves. I like to keep my relationship to this realm fairly private. In the beginning, it was important for me to check in with teachers, colleagues, and well-seasoned meditation facilitators, to help make sense of my efforts. Now that my connection to my Bliss Body is well-established and fully integrated into my daily living, I can enjoy the ride without worrying or wondering if I am doing it right or if my journey should look more like someone else's.

### Celebrate the Results

A life well-led is the ultimate celebration of the Bliss Body. When the connection becomes not something you do, but who you are, the experience is its own reward. In the early days, you can celebrate by creating a dedicated space adorned with items that bring you joy and spiritual connection.

"When you are compassionate with yourself, you trust in your soul, which you let guide your life. Your soul knows the geography of your destiny better than you do."

– *John O'Donohue*

# Conclusion

As my team and I were putting the final touches on this guide, I was going through a major life transition into a new, positive, and preferred state of being. My upbeat perspective was derailed, however, when I unexpectedly hit a stretch of significant stress and discontent. This perfectly human experience threw me into a place of immediate reaction as I was overwhelmed by deep feelings of disappointment and sadness.

Thankfully, the information shared through this guide was top of mind for me and I recognized this as a great opportunity to 'walk the walk' and put the concepts presented into action. Though still upset, I hit pause on life and planted myself on my meditation cushion. I was greeted by my homemade alter of icons, photos, and remembrances from travels past. Holding my string of mala beads (prayer beads from the Hindu tradition), I allowed myself to focus on the moment at hand. Some may call this meditation; some may call it prayer. I think of it as both.

I began by vocalizing all that I was grateful for, and then moved into a chant that is close to my heart. As I marked each round with a bead, my mind started to push through the feelings of fear and limitation that had been weighing me down and move into a place and space filled with light, a sense of safety and clarity. Soon I began to hear the whisperings of the Wisdom Body between the cadence of the chant. The messages were short and soothing, and I recognized them as what was Real and True (unlike the messages I had been hearing while burdened by reactionary feelings and thoughts). I was calmed by this inner knowing and I continued my practice until the last of the 108 beads were marked.

In the days following this meditation, I was able to feel and act more secure and upright and was open enough to start drawing on the strength and support of those around me. Had the stress and angst magically disappeared completely? Not quite, but I felt confident that time, grace, and many more sessions on my meditation cushion, would see me through.

Soren Kierkegaard, the famous Danish theologian, philosopher, and poet said, "The function of prayer is not to influence God, but rather to change the nature of the one who prays." This experience reminded me that the answers to everything we need to know are already inside us. It also laid bare how understanding and learning about the five layers of self can help us all through the toughest of times.

Taking care of others – to any degree, occasional or constant, by profession or voluntarily- can be an enervating effort. As caregivers, we can use the practices shared in this guide to infuse some life force into the mix. We owe it to ourselves to make sure that our own life experience is added to the list of priorities, and to follow through from a place of love and patience.

Just like anything worthwhile, self-care takes a bit of work. The payoff, however, is so great and so important that we can't afford to avoid the challenge. Once you lock into the flow of paying attention and responding to what you really need, you'll see the positive benefits and ripple effects throughout your life and the lives of those around you.

My intention for sharing the deeply meaningful philosophy of the five Koshas is to remind you that you are more than your physical body and loving yourself fully and completely requires much more than a bubble bath. By exploring different ways to make space, pierce the layers, create pathways, receive messages, and honor ourselves for who we truly are, we discover that we are all absolute radiant beings. I wish for each of us to experience that radiance, in every moment, on every level.

"Talk to yourself like you would to someone you love."

– *Brene Brown*

# About the Author

**JANE MAYER IS A STUDENT OF LIFE** and believes in passing on the wisdom and lessons learned through her unique set of experiences, struggles and personal triumphs. Committed to following her passions, her remarkable career path began with her working as a producer of TV commercials in NYC, where she reveled in the magic of living and working in one of the greatest cities in the world.

Jane M. Mayer

Her next step was transformational, as she chose to focus on family and raise her two incredible boys while diving deeply into the world of yoga and wellness. Never one to go halfway, Jane completed her 500-hr yoga teacher certification and taught for awhile before opening her own yoga and wellness centers where she offered classes, workshops, and holistic therapies.

While running her studio, Jane authored and taught a 200-hour yoga teacher training program, as well as produced a series of guided meditation recordings. She continues to teach advanced yoga and philosophy, as well as offer her Postures of

Consciousness workshop (based on the 'I AM Yoga' system), at the Southwest Institute of Healing Arts in Tempe, Arizona.

In 2018, Jane combined her entrepreneurial spirit with her passion for cuisine and founded Sweet Jane, an online business offering a variety of delicious gourmet hand pies... made by Jane herself! When she's not doing yoga, running workshops, writing life guides, baking, or cooking for her family, you can find Jane walking her dog Luke, faithfully hitting the gym to promote a healthy lifestyle, and smiling with gratitude for all the amazing experiences life has provided.

"How much good inside
a day? Depends how
good you live 'em."

– *Shel Silverstein*

# Acknowledgments

ANOTHER TEAM EFFORT FOR this second book in the series is worthy of appreciation.

Since *Helping Mom* was released, my previously acknowledged "partner-in-life" Denis, became even more official as my husband, and his continued support throughout the process of launching *Self-Care* in conjunction with our hosting a major event was unmatched. I discovered through that process how none of us operates in a vacuum and the progress of one does not occur without the reflection of another. We are lucky to have each other and acknowledge our blessings each day.

My continued gratitude goes to Margi Levitt of The Aspen Press, my faithful web and book designer and friend. I am so grateful to her for sticking with me through the many stops and starts, and for always being a positive, encouraging, intelligent and creative force in my life. I have other choices to create and self publish, but my relationship to her outweighs any efficiency that may be offered in another realm.

Stacey Dyck, who I now can refer to as "my editor" was referred to me for this project, and continues to be a gem! Thanks to her for keeping my voice and style intact while she worked to refine the content. Her feedback as an editor is important, but she also reported having been inspired to reconnect with her personal meditation practice after reading the book. That feedback is invaluable.

My old pal from NYC, Bob Giammarco, referred me to Steve Harrison at AE Media, who made quick work of the book's audio recording. I am lucky to have such a professional and highly tuned talent available to me.

"The challenge is not to be perfect – it is to be whole."

*– Jane Fonda*

www.ingramcontent.com/pod-product-compliance
Lightning Source LLC
Chambersburg PA
CBHW040035110426
42741CB00031B/107